The Little Christian's Songbook

Compiled by Daniel R. Burow
and Carol Greene

Drawings by Art Kirchhoff

CONCORDIA®

Publishing House
St. Louis

Concordia Publishing House, St. Louis, Missouri
Copyright © 1975 Concordia Publishing House
ISBN 0-570-03435-6

MANUFACTURED IN THE UNITED STATES OF AMERICA

contents

PRAISE him, PRAISE him!

Praise Him with trumpet sound!
Praise Him with lute and harp!
Praise Him with timbrel and dance;
Praise Him with strings and pipe!
Praise Him with sounding cymbals;
Praise Him with loud clashing cymbals!
Let everything that breathes praise the Lord!
Praise the Lord!

Psalm 150 RSV

You know, it just might be possible to plan an entire music curriculum with Psalm 150 as a guide. Enrollment practices could be determined by Psalm 148 — "young men and maidens together, old men and children." But that isn't why I chose to open this introduction with a psalm. Every introduction should be based on some well-defined presuppositions and, since the psalmist has already gone to all the trouble of clearly defining mine, it would be silly not to let him speak for himself.

Presupposition 1: It is good and fitting to praise God through music. Actually, a quick survey of other psalms will reveal that David and his fellow musicians felt that it was good and fitting to express many emotions to and about God through music. "In Thee, O Lord, do I seek refuge; let me never be put to shame." (Ps. 31:1) "Why do you boast, O mighty man, of mischief done against the godly?" (Ps. 52:1)

Presupposition 2: Small children can and should participate in musical expressions to and about God. Certainly children are a part of "everything that breathes." But their physical and temperamental characteristics especially suit them for actively making joyful noises.

In his book *From Two to Five* (Berkeley, University of California Press, 1971), the noted children's poet and observer of children Kornei Chukovsky speaks at length of the small child's fascination with and gravitation to rhyme and rhythm. As an example he cites the following chant spontaneously composed by a 4-year-old to annoy his sister:

I'm a big, big rider,
You're smaller than a spider.

Chukovsky also notes that small children do most of their chanting or versifying when they are moving around — chasing a soap bubble, hopping, or skipping. Small children don't lock their minds and voices off somewhere separate from their bodies; they say what they have to say with all of themselves. All of which means that actively involving small children in musical expression works better than having them sit quietly in their chairs and sing.

I recently asked a woman friend (who has her degree in music education and who teaches preschoolers) what her advice would be to grown-ups who wanted to make greater use of music with small children. Her immediate reply was: "Don't be afraid to try anything!" In explaining herself further, she shared the following two incidents:

Incident 1: The children had for some time been listening and moving to simple pieces by Bach, Kabalevsky, and other major composers. But one day the teacher decided to see how they would react to a Bach fugue (one of the most sophisticated musical forms around). She reminded them of puzzles they liked to play with, then explained that Bach liked to play with puzzles too—only his puzzles were in music. He liked to take a little melody and see how many ways he could play it in the same piece. She played the fugue's subject for them and then asked them to lie down, listen to the whole piece, and see if they could count all the times Bach used that melody. Two children came up with the exact total, a feat well beyond many college form-and-analysis classes!

Incident 2: The teacher had just returned from a month's visit to Japan and brought with her a number of recordings of Japanese folksongs, which she played for the children. They were delighted, quickly determined favorites, and asked to hear them again and again. Within a short time they had learned several —in Japanese and with no distinction between those songs originally intended for performance by children and those written for adults.

These incidents reminded me of an experience I had when I was working on the records included twice a year in HAPPY TIMES, a magazine for preschoolers. Each record included four songs, three that I considered suitable for small children to sing and one which told a Bible story and was really intended for listening purposes. To my surprise, many children ended up learning the Bible story song right along with the others. And they learned them all in the same way—by playing the record until the grooves had worn smooth and their parents had invested in earplugs. Repetition is no bane to small children; they delight in it and learn from it.

"Of course," my teacher friend confessed, "you will have some failures. And," she concluded, "you have to get right in there and participate with the children. Sing, play instruments, dance, move around. Your enthusiasm means a lot to them."

Now then, armed with valid presuppositions and encouraging incidents, what are some specifics you can try with your own small musicmakers?

1. Action addition: Children love action songs, as we all know. But what about all those songs that don't have actions to go with them? Add them. A few general questions to ask yourself first: (1) What will little children like to do? (2) What *can* they do? (3) What can they do in the space of a given musical line? "Little Jesus, Oh, So Small" (see p. 31) should be a good piece to practice on, because its words weren't really written to be accompanied by actions. And yet, actions are possible. For example:

"Little Jesus, Oh, so small" *(children reach down to indicate smallness);* "See Him sleeping in a manger" *(children rest heads on folded hands);* "Born to be the King of all" *(children reach up to indicate greatness);* "Born to save us all from danger" *(children spread arms to indicate everybody).*

Verse 2: "Little donkey, don't you cry" *(children point to imaginary donkey and shake heads);* "Sheep and lambs now still your bleating" *(children hold finger to lips);* "Peaceful let the Baby lie" *(children kneel down);* "Let Him sleep while night is fleeting" *(children rest heads on folded hands).*

2. Creative movement: Rather than telling the children what actions to perform, choose a lively song and invite them to make up their own motions to go with it. Explain to them that the person who wrote the music was praising God by putting beautiful sounds together, the person playing or singing the music is praising God by making the beautiful sounds happen with a musical instrument or voice, and they are praising God by moving to the beautiful sounds. Happy dance-like songs, songs with strong march rhythms, and slow dreamy pieces are all good for creative movement. If you can play the music yourself or talk someone else into doing it, all the better. But records work too.

If the words or music seem to suggest a theme for the movements, consider providing some costumes and props. Children love to march around the room to "Hosanna, Hosanna!" with cloths draped over their heads and construction paper palm branches. But sometimes just let them listen to the music and evolve their own theme. And don't forget to be there with them, evolving too.

3. Accompaniments: Many songs lend themselves to homegrown accompaniments. For example, look at "Christmas News" (p. 34). The children could either sing verse 1 or beat out tattoos of their own devising on coffee-can or oatmeal-carton drums. If you don't have a set of handbells, try jingle bells fastened to elastic bracelets for verse 2. And any kind of whistle should work for verse 3. None of the instruments require great financial outlay, and they can be used over and over with other songs.

4. New compositions: Let the children help you make up new words and actions to songs they already know. "Oh, Who Can Make a Flower?" can easily become "Oh, Who Can Make a Puppy?" And after you have the basic pattern established, the children can work with you on further verses.

"Oh, who can make . . . What are some other things God has made, Dennis?"

(No response—a little prompting is often necessary with small children.)

"Well, does God make robins? Right! Of course He does! Oh, who can make a robin, etc."

One advantage of this technique is that you can use it to suit the purposes of specific situations. "Praise Him, Praise Him," can be quickly transformed into "Thank Him, Thank Him," etc.

Some of the songs that follow already include suggestions for use; some don't. Feel free to adapt or ignore the suggestions and to provide your own wherever possible. Write them in the margins so you—or whoever next uses the book—will have them for reference.

And one final word of caution: Charming as the picture may be of orderly rows of spotlessly clad little songsters singing their portion of the Sunday school program perfectly in tune, it may represent only some nursery impresario's dream. Real children just don't function like that. They're noisy, and they wiggle. Better put away those dreams of aesthetic perfection and instead direct your energies to encouraging them in full-bodied, heartfelt expressions of themselves to God and about God through music.

Carol Greene

me and all creatures

"I believe that God has made me and all creatures . . ."
Martin Luther

he loves me

God Loves Me Dearly

1 God loves me dear - ly, Helps and for - gives me, God loves me
2 He sent forth Je - sus, That true Re - deem - er, He sent forth
3 Now will I praise Thee, O Love E - ter - nal; Now will I

dear - ly, Loves e - ven me.
Je - sus And set me free. There-fore I'll say a - gain: God loves me
praise Thee All my life long.

dear - ly, God loves me dear - ly, Loves e - ven me.

God's a Father Kind and True

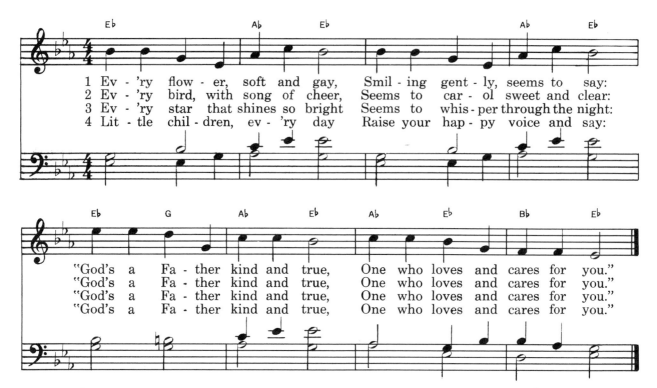

1 Ev-'ry flow-er, soft and gay, Smil-ing gent-ly, seems to say:
2 Ev-'ry bird, with song of cheer, Seems to car-ol sweet and clear:
3 Ev-'ry star that shines so bright Seems to whis-per through the night:
4 Lit-tle chil-dren, ev-'ry day Raise your hap-py voice and say:

"God's a Fa-ther kind and true, One who loves and cares for you."
"God's a Fa-ther kind and true, One who loves and cares for you."
"God's a Fa-ther kind and true, One who loves and cares for you."
"God's a Fa-ther kind and true, One who loves and cares for you."

Teaching suggestion: Let the children pretend to be flowers, birds, stars, and themselves with the appropriate verses.

God, Whose Name Is Love

Florence Hoatson

Haslemere

1 God, whose name is Love, Lit-tle ones are we!
2 Help us to be good, Al-ways kind and true,

Lis-ten to the hymns That we sing to Thee.
In the games we play Or the work we do.

God Is There

Carol Greene

Early American hymn

From the ear - ly morn - ing dew Till the last small star peeks through, God is there; ____ He's tak - ing care Of __ me and you. ____

Teaching suggestion: This song is fun to march to.

Sometimes

Carol Greene

Easily

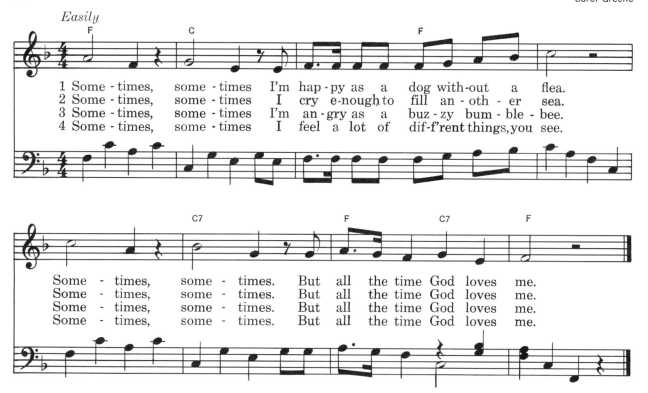

1 Some - times, some - times I'm hap - py as a dog with-out a flea.
2 Some - times, some - times I cry e-nough to fill an - oth - er sea.
3 Some - times, some - times I'm an - gry as a buz - zy bum - ble - bee.
4 Some - times, some - times I feel a lot of dif-f'rent things, you see.

Some - times, some - times. But all the time God loves me.
Some - times, some - times. But all the time God loves me.
Some - times, some - times. But all the time God loves me.
Some - times, some - times. But all the time God loves me.

Teaching suggestion: Let the children act out the emotions described in the first three verses. During the last verse they might dance or sway.

he made me

God Made Me

Daniel Burow

Bouncy

God made me, Ev - 'ry part you see:

Ears and eyes and mouth and nos - es, Feet that with so man - y toes - es

Skip and jump and hop, Al - most nev - er stop!

Teaching suggestion: Let the children point to the appropriate parts of their bodies. They might also skip, hop, or dance to the song.

I Can Stamp

G. A.

American folk song
Adapted Gretchen Anderson

Brightly

1 I can stamp and stamp my feet, Stamp my feet, Stamp my feet,
2 I can shake and shake my hands, Shake my hands, Shake my hands.
3 I can nod and nod my head, Nod my head, Nod my head.
4 I can wig - gle all of me, All of me, All of me.

I can stamp and stamp my feet. God gave me these feet.
I can shake and shake my hands. God gave me these hands.
I can nod and nod my head. God gave me this head.
I can wig - gle all of me. God made all of me.

Teaching suggestion: Let the children do the actions described.

I Can Do Lots of Things

C. G.

Carol Greene

1 I can build with my blocks tow-ers up to the sky. See my
2 I can paint pret-ty pic-tures in red, yel-low, blue. I can
4 I can think might-y thoughts, thoughts of cas-tles and kings. And of
5 I can do lots of things that an an-i-mal can't, Not a

blocks go-ing up al-most nine-ty feet high. Clop, clop, clop, clop,
paint on the pa-per and on me and you. Blob, blob, blob, blob,
pud-dles and poo-dles and noo-dles and things. *(Spoken:) Right now I'm going to think*
cow, not a goose, not a pig, not an ant. *(Spoken:) Want me to tell you why?*

clop, clop, clop, clop. Whoops! They fall down.
blob, blob, blob, blob. Whoops! In my lunch.
about a polar bear. Whoops! *(Spoken:) I thought about a porcupine too.*
It's not really a secret. God made me that way!

14

3 I can sing pret-ty songs with my mouth o-pen wide. I can
sing them so loud you can see my in-side. La la la la,
la la la! Whoops! Sang it wrong.

he made the whole world

Who Made the Sky So Bright and Blue?

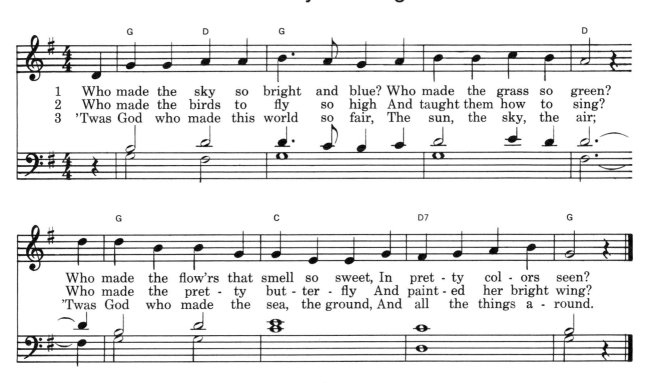

1 Who made the sky so bright and blue? Who made the grass so green?
2 Who made the birds to fly so high And taught them how to sing?
3 'Twas God who made this world so fair, The sun, the sky, the air;

Who made the flow'rs that smell so sweet, In pret-ty col-ors seen?
Who made the pret-ty but-ter-fly And paint-ed her bright wing?
'Twas God who made the sea, the ground, And all the things a-round.

All Things Bright and Beautiful

1 The cold winds in the win - ter, The pleas - ant sum - mer
2 He gave us eyes to see them, And lips that we might

sun, The ripe fruits in the au - tumn, God made them ev - 'ry one.
tell The good - ness of the Fa - ther, Who has made all things well.

REFRAIN

Yes, all things bright and beau - ti - ful, All crea - tures great and

small, And all things wise and won - der - ful, The Lord God made them all.

16

Oh, Who Can Make a Flower?

Grace W. Owens

Clara Lee Parker
Arr. Charlotte Mitchell

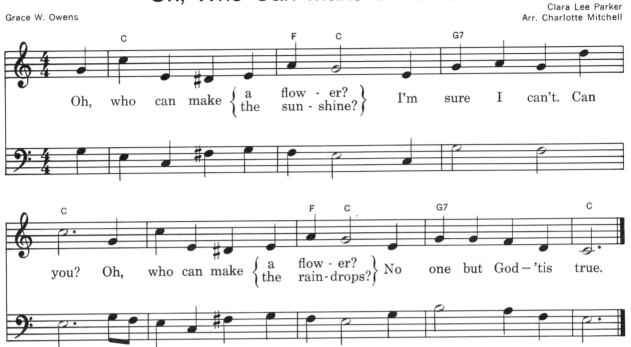

Oh, who can make { a flow-er? / the sun-shine? } I'm sure I can't. Can

you? Oh, who can make { a flow-er? / the rain-drops? } No one but God—'tis true.

Teaching suggestion: Help the children make up new verses.

The Springtime Calls to the Flowers

Mildred Adair

M. A.

The spring-time calls to the flow-ers, "Wake up, it's time to grow.___ I

want you to bright-en the world each day, Our Fa-ther's love to show."___

Teaching suggestion: Let the children pretend to be flowers—crouching down at the beginning of the song, then slowly rising.

Little Blue Flower

G. MacDonald, adapted

German folk tune
Arr. Charlotte Mitchell

Lyrics:

Lit - tle blue flow - er sat next to a stone,
Droop-ing and wait - ing un - til the sun shone.
Lit - tle blue flow - er with sun - shine was fed.
Lit - tle blue flow - er is lift - ing her head.

Lit - tle blue flow - er is droop-ing with pain,
Wait - ing and wait - ing for nour-ish - ing rain;
Lit - tle blue flow - er is hold - ing her cup.
Rain is fast fall - ing and fill - ing it up.

Lit - tle blue flow - er now smells ver - y sweet,
On her head sun - shine and rain at her feet.
Thanks to the sun-shine, and thanks to the rain!
Lit - tle blue flow - er is hap - py a - gain.

Teaching suggestion: Let the children act out this song.

18

A Great Gray Elephant

Helen C. Dykema

A great gray el-e-phant, A lit-tle yel-low bee, A ti-ny pur-ple vi-o-let, A tall green tree, A red and white sail-boat on a blue sea: All these things You gave to me When You made my eyes to see; All these things You gave to me. Thank You, God!

Courtesy of the National Society for the Prevention of Blindness

Teaching suggestion: Let the children draw pictures of the items mentioned in this song.

Summertime Is Here Now

Daniel Burow

Traditional German

1 Sum - mer - time is here now; School is out all day.
2 Trees are green and shad - y By the swings and slide.
3 I can splash at sea - shores Or in hy - drant spray.

Thank You, God, for sum - mer: Time for out - door play.
When I play out - side.
What a time for play!

La - la - la, la - la - la, la - la - la - la. La - la, la - la - la - la - la.

La - la - la, la - la - la, la - la - la - la. La - la, la - la - la - la - la.

Teaching suggestion: This song is a good one for dancing or swaying.

Red, Yellow, Brown

Carol Greene

German folk tune

Rhythmically

Red, yel - low, brown. See them fall down. Bright leaves are fill - ing the air.
God makes them fall, Cov - er - ing all. Each lit - tle leaf seems to know

Soon all the trees will be bare. Red, yel - low, brown. See them fall down.
Next spring a new one will grow. God makes them fall, Cov - er - ing all.

Teaching suggestion: Let the children pretend to be leaves and dance around.

God's Winter Love

E. S.

Elizabeth Sparrow

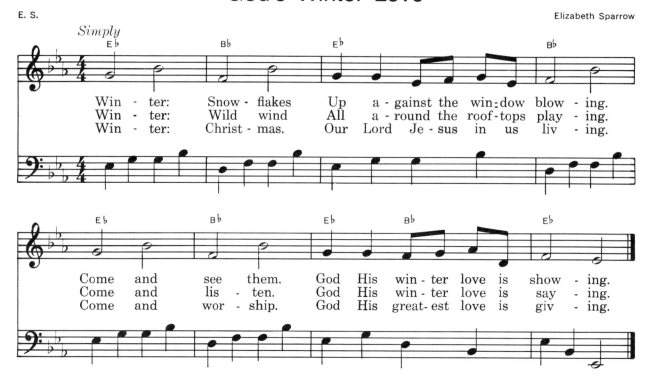

Win - ter: Snow - flakes Up a - gainst the win-dow blow - ing.
Win - ter: Wild wind All a - round the roof-tops play - ing.
Win - ter: Christ - mas. Our Lord Je - sus in us liv - ing.

Come and see them. God His win - ter love is show - ing.
Come and lis - ten. God His win - ter love is say - ing.
Come and wor - ship. God His great-est love is giv - ing.

thank you, god!
Praise Him, Praise Him

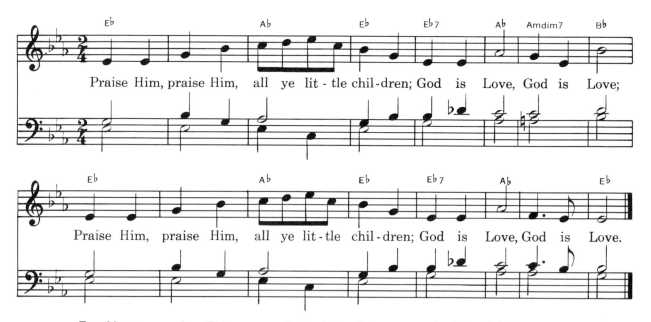

Praise Him, praise Him, all ye lit - tle chil-dren; God is Love, God is Love;

Praise Him, praise Him, all ye lit - tle chil-dren; God is Love, God is Love.

Teaching suggestion: This song easily lends itself to new words: "Thank Him," "Love Him," "Tell Him," etc.

Thank You, Loving Father

Verses 1-4 Arthur W. Gross
Verses 5-6 Daniel Burow

Arr. Theo. J. Koch

1 God made all the food we eat;
3 God made all the birds that sing; Thank You, lov - ing Fa - ther.
5 God made me and God made you;

2 God made all the flow'rs so sweet;
4 God made us and ev - 'ry - thing; Thank You, lov - ing Fa - ther.
6 God made fa - thers, moth - ers too;

Praise and Thanks

Carol Greene

Franz Joseph Haydn

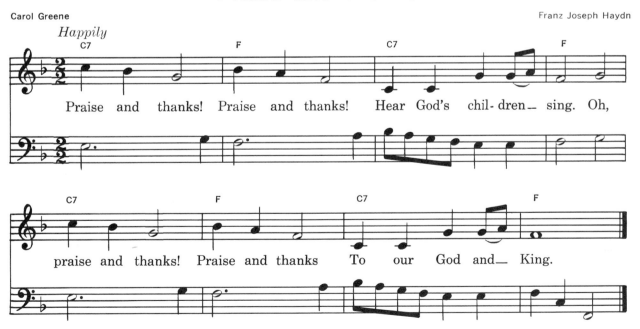

Praise and thanks! Praise and thanks! Hear God's chil - dren sing. Oh,

praise and thanks! Praise and thanks To our God and King.

Song of Thanks

C. G.

Hungarian folk song
Arr. Carol Greene

Gently

Heav - en - ly Fa - ther, hear us say   Our spe-cial

thanks to You this day: Thanks for all the love You

send our way,   And for Your Son, Je - sus, thanks we pay.

Teaching suggestion: This song might be used as a table grace.

24

that I may BE his

"I believe that Jesus Christ, true God . . . and also true man . . . has redeemed me . . . that I may be His own, and live under Him in His kingdom, and serve Him in everlasting righteousness, innocence, and blessedness."

Martin Luther

he's my friend

Jesus Is My Special Friend

Daniel Burow

Carol Greene

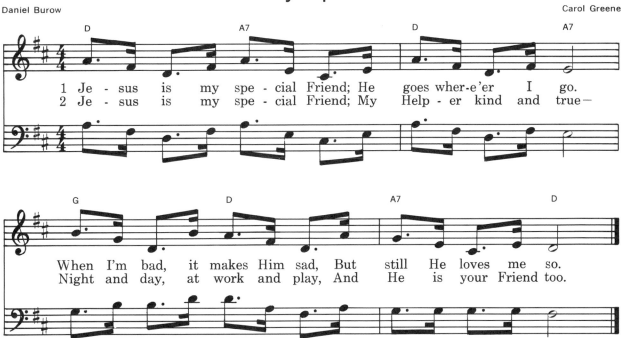

1 Je - sus is my spe - cial Friend; He goes wher-e'er I go.
2 Je - sus is my spe - cial Friend; My Help - er kind and true—

When I'm bad, it makes Him sad, But still He loves me so.
Night and day, at work and play, And He is your Friend too.

Teaching suggestion: This song is especially good for skipping or dancing.

My Friend Jesus

Carol Greene

Franz Schubert

Slowly

1 My Friend Je - sus, He is al - ways here be - side me;
2 My Friend Je - sus, Loves me e - ven when I'm naugh - ty;
3 I love Je - sus. I know He's my Friend for - ev - er.

Loves me, cares for me, Lis - tens to me when I pray.
Takes my sins a - way, Helps me start a - gain each day.
I am His friend too, And His friend I'll al - ways stay.

Jesus Loves Me, This I Know

Anna B. Warner

William B. Bradbury
Arr. Charlotte Mitchell

1 Je - sus loves me, this I know, For the Bi - ble tells me so;
2 Je - sus loves me, He who died Heav-en's gate to o - pen wide;

Lit - tle ones to Him be - long, They are weak, but He is strong.
He will wash a - way my sin, Let His lit - tle child come in.

REFRAIN

Yes, Je - sus loves me! Yes, Je - sus loves me!

Yes, Je - sus loves me! The Bi - ble tells me so.

In the Morning

G. A.

Gretchen Anderson

Brightly

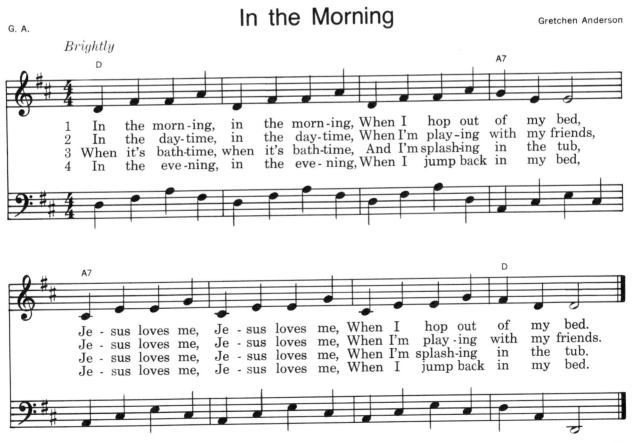

1 In the morn-ing, in the morn-ing, When I hop out of my bed,
2 In the day-time, in the day-time, When I'm play-ing with my friends,
3 When it's bath-time, when it's bath-time, And I'm splash-ing in the tub,
4 In the eve-ning, in the eve-ning, When I jump back in my bed,

Je - sus loves me, Je - sus loves me, When I hop out of my bed.
Je - sus loves me, Je - sus loves me, When I'm play-ing with my friends.
Je - sus loves me, Je - sus loves me, When I'm splash-ing in the tub.
Je - sus loves me, Je - sus loves me, When I jump back in my bed.

Jesus Loves the Little Children

Arr. Charlotte Mitchell

Je - sus loves the lit - tle chil - dren, All the chil - dren of the
Je - sus died for all the chil - dren, All the chil - dren of the

world; Red and yel - low, black and white, All are pre - cious in His
world; Red and yel - low, black and white, All are pre - cious in His

sight: Je - sus loves the lit - tle chil - dren of the world.
sight: Je - sus died for all the chil - dren of the world.

he came to earth

Jesus, Our Good Friend

C. G.

Carol Greene
Arr. Charlotte Mitchell

Happily

Some-one's com - ing, Some-one spe-cial, Je - sus, our good Friend;____
See the star that shines to wel-come Je - sus, our good Friend;____
He was once a child like I am, Je - sus, our good Friend;____
He grew up the same as I will, Je - sus, our good Friend;____

Soon He'll be a lit - tle ba - by, Je - sus, our good Friend.____
See, it leads the peo - ple to Him, Je - sus, our good Friend.____
Work - ing, play - ing, learn - ing, lov - ing, Je - sus, our good Friend.____
Went to show the world God loves them, Je - sus, our good Friend.____

Away in a Manger

Traditional

1 A - way in a man - ger, no crib for a bed, The
2 The cat - tle are low - ing, the Ba - by a - wakes, But
3 Be near me, Lord Je - sus, I ask Thee to stay Close

lit - tle Lord Je - sus laid down His sweet head; The
lit - tle Lord Je - sus, no cry - ing He makes. I
by me for - ev - er, and love me, I pray. Bless

stars in the sky —— looked down where He lay, The
love in Thee, Lord Je - sus, look down from the sky, And
all the dear chil - dren in Thy ten - der care, And

lit - tle Lord Je - sus, a - sleep on the hay.
stay by my side un - til morn - ing is nigh.
take us to heav - en, to live with Thee there.

Little Jesus, Oh, So Small

Carol Greene

Robert Schumann

Gently

1 Lit - tle Je - sus, oh, so small,
2 Lit - tle don - key, don't you cry.

See Him sleep - ing in a man - ger, Born to be the
Sheep and lambs, now still your bleat - ing. Peace - ful let the

King of all, Born to save us all from dan - ger.
Ba - by lie. Let Him sleep while night is fleet - ing.

The Friendly Beasts

12th-Century English

1 Je - sus, our Broth - er, kind and good, Was hum - bly
2 "I," said the don - key, shag - gy and brown, "I car - ried His
3 "I," said the cow, all white and red, "I gave Him my

born in a sta - ble rude, And the friend - ly beasts a -
moth - er, up hill and down; I car - ried His moth - er to
man - ger for His bed, I gave Him my hay to

round Him stood; Je - sus, our Broth - er, kind and good.
Beth - le - hem town!" "I," said the don - key, shag - gy and brown.
pil - low His head." "I," said the cow, all white and red.

Teaching suggestion: Let the children pretend to be a donkey and a cow as they sing the appropriate verses.

Hush, Not a Peep

Daniel Burow, tr.

Salzburg Christmas carol

Lightly, tenderly

1 Hush! ___ Not a peep! The ___ Christ Child ___ needs to ___
2 Sleep, ___ sleep, ___ sleep, My ___ lit - tle ___ Je - sus, ___

sleep. Hear Mar - y ___ sing - ing songs so ___ sweet - ly
sleep. The an - gel ___ choir with mut - ed ___ voic - es

As she ___ feeds our Lord so ___ meek - ly. Hush! ___ Not a
Round the ___ sleep - y Child re - joic - es. Sleep, ___ sleep, ___

peep! The ___ Christ Child ___ needs to ___ sleep.
sleep, My ___ lit - tle Je - sus ___ sleep.

Little Children, Can You Tell?

1 Lit - tle chil - dren, can you tell, Do you know the
2 Yes, we know the sto - ry well; Lis - ten now, and
3 For a lit - tle Babe that day Cra - dled in a

sto - ry well, Ev - 'ry girl and ev - 'ry boy, Why the an - gels
hear us tell, Ev - 'ry girl and ev - 'ry boy, Why the an - gels
man - ger lay. Born on earth our Lord to be; This the won - d'ring

sing for joy On the Christ - mas morn - ing?
sing for joy On the Christ - mas morn - ing.
an - gels see On the Christ - mas morn - ing.

Christmas News

C. G.

Carol Greene

Happily

1 Hear us sing; News we bring: Je - sus the Sav - ior is born! —
2 Hear the bell; Here it tell: Je - sus the Sav - ior is born! —
3 Hear the bird Spread the word: Je - sus the Sav - ior is born! —

Hear us sing; News we bring: Je-sus the Sav-ior is born!
Hear the bell; Hear it tell: Je-sus the Sav-ior is born!
Hear the bird Spread the word: Je-sus the Sav-ior is born!

Oh, Come, Little Children

Christian v. Schmid
Tr. unknown

Johann Abraham Peter Schulz

1 Oh, come, lit-tle chil-dren, oh, come, one and all, To Beth-le-hem
2 He's born in a sta-ble for you and for me; Draw near by the
3 See Ma-ry and Jo-seph, with love-beam-ing eyes, Are gaz-ing up-
4 Kneel down and a-dore Him with shep-herds to-day, Lift up lit-tle

haste to the man-ger so small. God's Son for a gift has been
bright, gleam-ing star-light to see, In swad-dling clothes ly - ing, so
on the rude bed where He lies; The shep-herds are kneel-ing, with
hands now and praise Him as they; Re - joice that a Sav-ior from

sent you this night To be your Re - deem - er, your Joy, and De - light.
meek and so mild, And pur - er than an - gels, the heav-en-ly Child.
hearts full of love, While an - gels sing loud al - le - lu - ias a - bove.
sin you can boast, And join in the song of the heav - en - ly host.

he lived with us

Young Jesus Grew in Naz'reth

Daniel Burow

German folk melody

Young Je-sus grew in Naz-'reth, Was gen-tle as a dove;____ He *went to school,* like I do; He loved as God a-bove.____

*played fun games
learned of God
ate His meals
said His prayers

washed His face
scraped His knees
cried when hurt
ran outdoors

helped at home
shared His toys
slept at night

36

Jump! Shout!

Carol Greene
Arr. Charlotte Mitchell

C. G.

Jump! Shout! Spin your-self a - bout! Clap your hands and sing a

song! Je - sus was a good Friend long a - go in Ga - li - lee. And

He is still a good Friend now to you and to me.   1 Mat-thew was a
                                                   2 Je - sus told a
                                                   3 Zac - chae-us was a

naugh - ty man, as grum - py as could be. Till
sto - ry of a boy who ran a - way. He
lit - tle man, a lit - tle man was he. He

Je - sus said, "Hey, Mat - thew! Come a - long and fol - low Me!" Then
did - n't want to work and thought he'd go some-place and play. But
want - ed to see Je - sus so he climbed in - to a tree. Now,

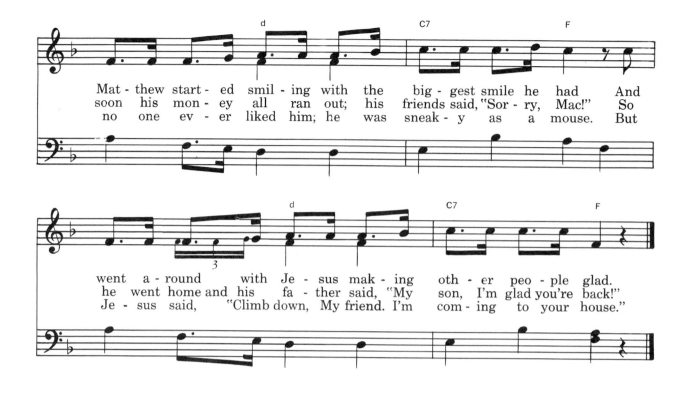

Mat - thew start - ed smil - ing with the big - gest smile he had. And
soon his mon - ey all ran out; his friends said, "Sor - ry, Mac!" So
no one ev - er liked him; he was sneak - y as a mouse. But

went a - round with Je - sus mak - ing oth - er peo - ple glad.
he went home and his fa - ther said, "My son, I'm glad you're back!"
Je - sus said, "Climb down, My friend. I'm com - ing to your house."

he died and rose again

Hosanna, Hosanna!

Carol Greene

L. v. Beethoven
Arr. Charlotte Mitchell

Ho - san - na, ho - san - na! Oh, hear the chil - dren sing!

Ho - san - na, ho - san - na! To Je - sus Christ, their King.

There Is a Green Hill Far Away

Verses 1 and 3 Cecil Francis Alexander
Verses 2 and 4 Daniel Burow

William Horsley

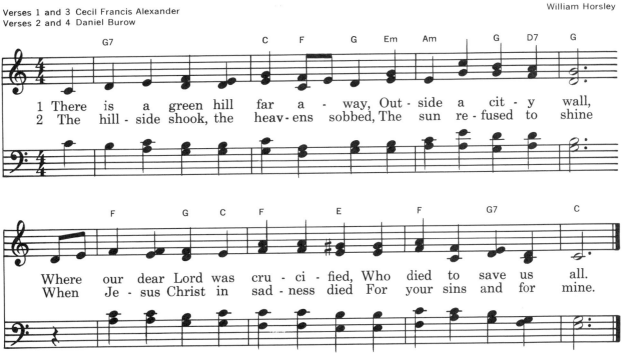

1 There is a green hill far a - way, Out - side a cit - y wall,
2 The hill - side shook, the heav - ens sobbed, The sun re - fused to shine

Where our dear Lord was cru - ci - fied, Who died to save us all.
When Je - sus Christ in sad - ness died For your sins and for mine.

3 We may not know, we cannot tell,
What pains He had to bear,
But we believe it was for us
He hung and suffered there.

4 He loved us then, He loves us still,
Oh, may we love Him too
And show each day we are His friends
By all we say and do.

39

On the Cross

Sarah Fletcher

Elizabeth Sparrow

Simply

On the cross_ of Cal - va - ry, Dear - est Lord, You died for me.

Help me, Lord; my sins for - give. Teach me, Lord,_ like You to live.

My Savior Lives

Carol Greene

L. v. Beethoven, adapted

Happily

My Sav - ior lives! My Sav - ior lives! He loves me

so and al - ways stays be - side me. My Sav - ior lives! My

Sav - ior lives! I take His hand, for He will al - ways guide me.

Easter Joy

D. B.

Daniel Burow

Sing, O birds, your Eas - ter greet - ing: "Tweet, tweet," Oh, how sweet!

Praise the Lord, by whom you're fed; Ring, O bells, in rhyth - m

beat - ing: Ding, dong, With our song: "Je - sus lives, who once was dead."

Christ the Lord Is Risen Today

Robert Williams

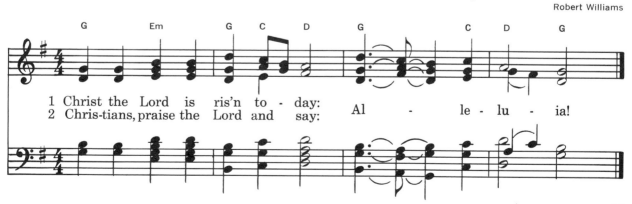

1 Christ the Lord is ris'n to - day: Al - le - lu - ia!
2 Chris-tians, praise the Lord and say:

newness of life

"We were buried with Him by Baptism into death, so that as Christ was raised from the dead by the glory of the Father, we too might walk in newness of life."

St. Paul (Rom. 6:4)

a community of love
In My Family

E. S.

Elizabeth Sparrow

In my fam-i-ly, in my fam-i-ly God gave me a { moth - er. / fa - ther. / grand - ma. }

For my fam-i-ly, for my fam-i-ly, Thank You, thank You, God.

Teaching suggestion: The children can fill in the blank to suit the composition of their own families.

I Have a Friend

I have a friend and a good friend too,
I have a friend and a good friend too, I have a friend and a
good friend too; Thank God for friends like you.

I Forgive

E. S.

Elizabeth Sparrow

Lively

1 When I hurt my friend, I feel sor-ry. And I say, "Please for-give."
2 When I do bad things, I hurt Je-sus. And I pray, "Please for-give."

When my friend hurts me, he feels sor-ry. And guess what? I for-give.
And I'm ver-y sure that His an-swer Al-ways is, "I for-give."

Our Church Family

E. S.

Elizabeth Sparrow

Brightly

1 Our church fam - i - ly meets to learn God's Word. _____
2 Our church fam - i - ly meets to sing and pray. _____
3 Our church fam - i - ly tries to show God's love. _____

Big, small, we all meet to learn God's Word.
Big, small, we all meet to sing and pray.
Big, small, we all try to show God's love.

I'm Glad

Carol Greene

German folk tune

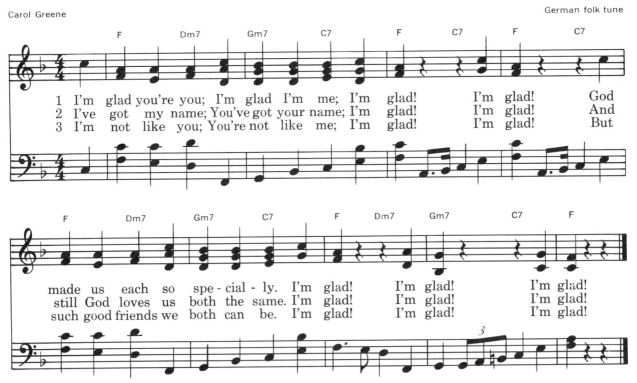

1 I'm glad you're you; I'm glad I'm me; I'm glad! I'm glad! God
2 I've got my name; You've got your name; I'm glad! I'm glad! And
3 I'm not like you; You're not like me; I'm glad! I'm glad! But

made us each so spe - cial - ly. I'm glad! I'm glad! I'm glad!
still God loves us both the same. I'm glad! I'm glad! I'm glad!
such good friends we both can be. I'm glad! I'm glad! I'm glad!

Teaching suggestion: The children might point to the appropriate persons while singing this song; they could also clap on the rests.

If You Feel Happy

C. G.   Carol Greene

1 If you feel hap - py,   If you feel hap - py,
2 If you feel sad, ___   If you feel sad, ___
3 If you feel grump - y,   If you feel grump - y,
4 If you feel fright - ened,   If you feel fright - ened,
5 If you feel lov - ing,   If you feel lov - ing,

If you feel hap - py,   Clap your hands with me. (Clap! Clap!)
If you feel sad, ___   Cry a - long with me. (Boo-hoo!)
If you feel grump - y,   Shout it out with me. (Oh, rats!)
If you feel fright - ened,   Knock your knees with me. (Clop! Clop!)
If you feel lov - ing,   Hug a friend with me. (Mmmm!)

45

a community to help

God's Helpers Ev'rywhere

E. S.

Elizabeth Sparrow

Happily

God's help-ers ev - 'ry - where. God's help-ers ev - 'ry - where.

{ The
{ The
{ The

teach - er, the teach - er.
pas - tor, the pas - tor. } God's help-ers ev - 'ry - where.
doc - tor, the doc - tor.

I Want to Be a Helper

Verse 1 Mildred Adair
Verse 2 Daniel Burow

J. C. Wohlfeil

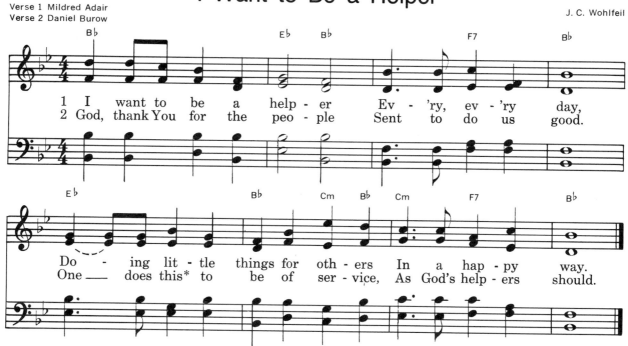

1 I want to be a help - er Ev - 'ry, ev - 'ry day,
2 God, thank You for the peo - ple Sent to do us good.

Do - ing lit - tle things for oth - ers In a hap - py way.
One ___ does this* to be of ser - vice, As God's help - ers should.

* Invent an action. After the verse the children can try to guess who the helper is. At other times the children may name a helper before singing the verse. In this case substitute the name of the helper for the word "One." For example, "Doctors do this . . ."

I Am Jesus' Helper

Carol Greene

Tyrolean melody

1 Though I'm not ver - y big, I am Je - sus' help - er.
2 Make oth - ers hap - py, Tell - ing them He loves_ them;

Though I'm not ver - y big, I can help Him too. too.
Make oth - ers hap - py, Lov - ing them too. too.

I Can Tell

G. A.

Gretchen Anderson

Happily

1 I can tell. I can tell. Lis - ten close - ly. I can tell.
2 Je - sus loves You and me. Can you hear me? I can tell.
3 We are His, Ev - 'ry one. Hear me say it. I can tell.
4 Je - sus died, Rose a - gain. What good news! Oh, I can tell.

HE HELPS US THROUGH PRAYER

I Talk to You, Jesus

Carol Greene

German folk song

Happily

1 I talk to You, Je - sus, Man - y times ev - 'ry day. I
2 Take care of me, Je - sus, And of all my friends too. Help

know You are lis - t'ning An - y time that I pray.
us to be hap - py And to al - ways love You.

Good Morning, God!

E. S.

Elizabeth Sparrow

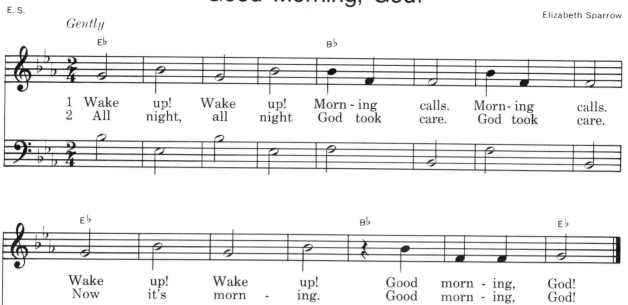

Gently

Eb   Bb

1 Wake up! Wake up! Morn - ing calls. Morn - ing calls.
2 All night, all night God took care. God took care.

Eb   Bb   Eb

Wake up! Wake up!   Good morn - ing, God!
Now it's morn - ing. Good morn - ing, God!

Good Night

Victor Hugo

Carol Greene

Gently

G   D   G   D

Good night! Good night! Far flies the light; But still God's love

G   D   D7   G

Shall shine a - bove, Mak - ing all bright; Good night! Good night!

Father, Hear Your Little Children

Daniel Burow

D. S. Bortniansky

Fa - ther, hear Your lit - tle chil - dren; Bless us in our school to - day.

Help us grow in love and kind - ness, More like Je - sus ev - 'ry day.

More like Je - sus! More like Je - sus! More like Je - sus ev - 'ry day!

Table Prayer

E. S.

Elizabeth Sparrow

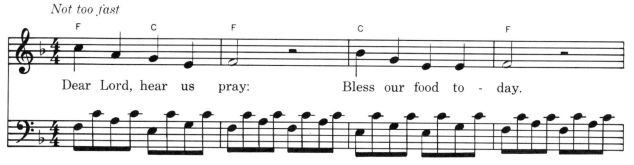

Dear Lord, hear us pray: Bless our food to - day.

Lord, we pray a - gain: _____ Bless us too. A - men.

Tender Jesus

Gretchen Anderson

Ten - der Je - sus, meek and mild, Look on me, a lit - tle child.

Help me, if it is Your will, To re - cov - er from all ill.

he helps us through his book

What a Wonderful World!

Carol Greene

Franz Schubert
Arr. Charlotte Mitchell

Not too fast

1 Ad - am sat up straight and looked a - round To __ see what he __ could __ see. "I must look at this new
2 God said, "Ad - am, here's a job for you. You will be a ver - y bus - y man. Will you please name all my
3 Ad - am felt a lit - tle lone - ly, though. He __ wished he had a peo - ple friend. So God made him go to
4 The __ world is ve - ry pret - ty, God. We __ like our bod - ies __ too. We __ want to thank You

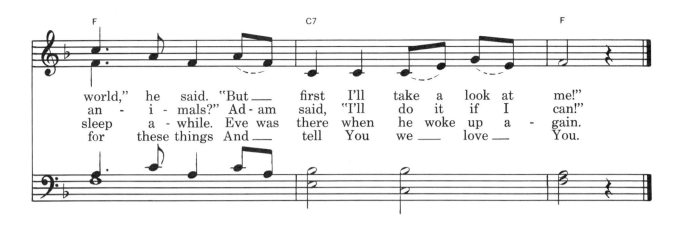

world," he said. "But first I'll take a look at me!"
an - i - mals?" Ad - am said, "I'll do it if I can!"
sleep a - while. Eve was there when he woke up a - gain.
for these things And tell You we love You.

Joseph's Song

Carol Greene

Franz Joseph Haydn
Arr. Charlotte Mitchell

Not too slow

1 Young Jo - seph had a pret - ty coat That made his broth - ers say:
2 So Jo - seph went to E - gypt land, He worked hard ev - 'ry day.
3 Then God made Jo - seph ver - y rich, He made the broth - ers poor;
4 "Well, come in, broth - ers!" Jo - seph cried; "I'll give you all you need.

"Since Fa - ther likes young Jo - seph best, Let's send him far a - way."
But he knew God was with him there And lis - t'ning to him pray.
And one day Jo - seph heard them all Come knock - ing at his door.
God wants us to be friends a - gain." His broth - ers all a - greed.

Moses

Carol Greene

Hungarian folk song
Arr. Charlotte Mitchell

1 Mo - ses boy, Sleep-ing on the Nile. Mo - ses boy,
2 Mo - ses man, God is call-ing you. Mo - ses man,
3 Mo - ses man, Though the jour-ney's hard, Mo - ses man,
4 Mo - ses man, Ca-naan lies be - low. Mo - ses man,

In a lit - tle while Phar-aoh's daugh-ter's com - ing.
Here's what you must do. Lead your cap - tive peo - ple
You can trust your Lord. See the Red Sea part - ing;
Let your peo - ple go. Now the jour - ney's o - ver;

She'll take you home. God is watch-ing o - ver. You're not a - lone.
Out of that land. Lead them home to Ca - naan, Mo - ses man.
Walk right on through. God is with His peo - ple; God is with you.
You've done your best. With God's help you made it; Now you can rest.

Sing, David, Sing

Carol Greene

14th-century English

Da - vid sang as he sat in the mead - ow. Sing, Da-vid, sing, Da-vid, prais - es to God! As you watch o - ver your sheep in the mead - ow, Sing, Da-vid, sing, Da-vid, prais - es to God!

Daniel and the Lions

Carol Greene

Franz Schubert

Not too fast

1 Old Dan - iel loved to pray to God. He did it ev - 'ry day.
2 Then Dan - iel an - swered, "I will pray! You can - not make me quit!"
3 The pit was full of hun - gry lions, And Dan - iel spent the night.
4 The king got Dan - iel out next day, Sur - prised he was - n't dead.

But then some bad men made a rule: "You can no long - er _ pray."
The an - gry men said, "All right, then! We'll throw you in a _ pit."
But God pro - tec - ted him and shut the li - ons' mouths up _ tight.
"I prayed, and God took care of me," was what old Dan - iel _ said.

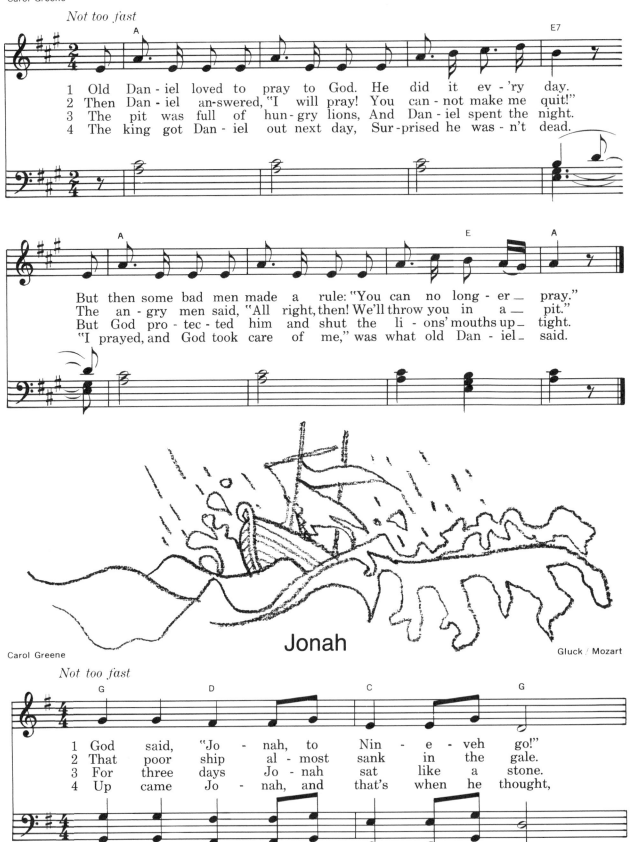

Jonah

Carol Greene

Gluck / Mozart

Not too fast

1 God said, "Jo - nah, to Nin - e - veh go!"
2 That poor ship al - most sank in the gale.
3 For three days Jo - nah sat like a stone.
4 Up came Jo - nah, and that's when he thought,

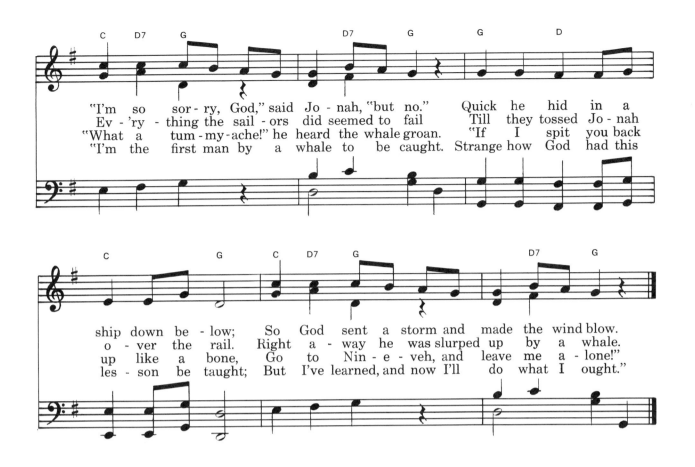

"I'm so sor - ry, God," said Jo - nah, "but no." Quick he hid in a
Ev - 'ry - thing the sail - ors did seemed to fail Till they tossed Jo - nah
"What a tum - my-ache!" he heard the whale groan. "If I spit you back
"I'm the first man by a whale to be caught. Strange how God had this

ship down be - low; So God sent a storm and made the wind blow.
o - ver the rail. Right a - way he was slurped up by a whale.
up like a bone, Go to Nin - e - veh, and leave me a - lone!"
les - son be taught; But I've learned, and now I'll do what I ought."

A Little Woolly Lamb

Carol Greene

W. A. Mozart

Easily

1 A lit - tle wool - ly lamb Went run - ning off pell -
2 The shep - herd looked a - round, Said, "Wool - ly lamb is
3 He found the wool - ly lamb By fol - low - ing his

mell. Then he got lost, And night - time fell.
lost. I'll find my lamb At an - y cost."
track. The oth - er sheep Said, "Wel - come back!"

Peter

E. S.

Elizabeth Sparrow

There was a man named Pe - ter, and Je - sus' friend was he. He

{fol-lowed / taught of} Je - sus ev - 'ry-where on land and on sea. Hey there, Pe - ter!

Je - sus' good friend. Hey there, Pe - ter! There he goes a - gain.

Paul

Carol Greene

W. A. Mozart

Rhythmically

1 When— Paul was a young man, He — was ver - y
2 Then — Je - sus came to him; Said,— "Paul, be My
3 So— Paul told of Je - sus In — lands far and

bad.   He — chased all the Chris - tian folk and made them sad.
friend." And — Paul said, "I will, my Lord. My ways I'll mend."
wide   And be - gan chur - ches ev - 'ry-where be - fore he died.

he helps us with his spirit

Here, There

E. S.

Elizabeth Sparrow

Happily

Here, there, ev - 'ry - where, In the day - time, in the night-time,
Here, there, ev - 'ry - where, When I'm work - ing, when I'm play - ing,
Here, there, ev - 'ry - where, With my play-mates, with my fam - 'ly

Here, there, ev - 'ry - where, God's Spir - it stays with me.
Here, there, ev - 'ry - where, God's Spir - it helps me grow.
Here, there, ev - 'ry - where, God's Spir - it helps me love.

OTHER SONGS

Birthday Song

E. S.

Elizabeth Sparrow

Hap-py birth-day! Hap-py birth-day! Hap-py birth-day to

you. Hap-py birth-day, dear * * And may God bless you too!

Hear Me Sing

E S.

L. v. Beethoven / Elizabeth Sparrow

1 Hear me sing my prais - es strong and true
2 "Dear - est Lord, be with me all day through

To my dear Friend: "Oh, Je - sus, I love You!"
And help me show Your love in all I do."

Teaching suggestion: This song might be used while presenting the offering.

Opening Song

E. S.

Elizabeth Sparrow

1 To - geth - er, Lord, we pray: Be with us here to - day.
2 Help us to be like You In all we say and do.

Make each of us Your Friend. ___ On each Your bless - ing send.
Oh, teach us to be kind. ___ Fill ev - 'ry heart _ and mind.

Goodbye, Goodbye

Elizabeth Sparrow

Brightly

Good - bye, good - bye, good - bye,— Good - bye, my friends, to you. God

bless you ev -'ry - where you go, In all you say and do.

62

index of first lines and titles